PAUSES FOR THE VACATIONING SOUL

A SENSORY-BASED DEVOTION GUIDE FOR THE BEACH

CATHY BAKER

FREE E-BOOK

FOREWORD

When Cathy Baker mentioned her idea to me of vacation-focused devotionals, my reaction was overwhelmingly positive!

First, Cathy is refreshing as a sister in Christ and as a writer. Her perspective is genuine, creative, and grounded in God's Word. I visit her blog whenever I need a fresh thought on my spiritual life. And her love for the Lord and for others, as well as her funny bone, inspires me all the time in our friendship.

Second, whenever I have an opportunity to get away, I desperately want a break from routine, but I'm not interested in a "getaway" from God! I love the idea of having a special devotional just for those times when I'm looking for a change from daily life. I always want to include God even when I'm on retreat or vacation, and this unconventional little book is just the ticket. Cathy's careful, but delightful approach to God's Word and spiritual life is a perfect match for this. She's a gentle soul willing to speak truth and light in an often dark world.

What you hold in your hand carries the scent of heaven and promises to accompany you to a place where God wants to share and to bless your fun, rest, and re-creation.

Lori Stanley Roeleveld, author of *Jesus and the Beanstalk (Overcoming Your Giants and Living a Fruitful Life)* and *Running from a Crazy Man (and Other Adventures Traveling with Jesus)*

INTRODUCTION

It began a few summers ago—the rousing within my spirit that vacation could mean more than unpacking, eating seafood, slathering up, and heading home with sandy particles in my suitcase.

The truth is, I was minding my own business at the time. A rented beach umbrella provided the perfect prop for a relaxing afternoon by the ocean. I felt the granules shifting beneath my feet and caught the scent of freshly sprayed oil on my skin. The glints from shiny shells mingling with the opaque were swoon-worthy. Gratitude washed over me as I reflected on God's sensory gifts.

These gifts enable us to see the vastness of the ocean, taste fresh seafood, and hear waves crash onto the shore. We can pick up seashells and feel their tumbled-worn edges. We can inhale deeply to capture the scent of sweet sea spray. And we can engage the soul, drawing us closer to God.

Pauses for the Vacationing Soul is an invitation to be still and know God—by experience—through what you see, taste, smell, touch, and hear.

It is an invitation to reawaken your senses to the wonder of God.

≈

HE QUIETED THE SEA WITH HIS POWER.
JOB 26:12A NASB

ARRIVAL DAY // PAUSE TO PREPARE

Heavenly Father,
Thank you for this vacation, for this gift of rest.
Show me how to savor every single moment this time away holds.
Open my eyes physically and spiritually to see You anew.
Awaken my ability to receive all You have for me,
one breath at a time.
Unlock my ears to hear You with divine clarity.
Brighten my spiritual taste buds to fully savor Your goodness.
Use everything I see, smell, hear, taste, and touch
for Your glory this week.
Amen.

If your beach vacation is anything like mine, arrival day involves unloading luggage, toys, and multiple boxes of food that include favorite munchies (as if the local grocery store doesn't carry them!), bottled water, and basic ingredients for meals. It's hectic, but anticipation quickly overrides the exhaustion.

1

Once the kitchen is stocked and my secret snacks are quietly stowed away in our room (it's an only child thing), I make my way outside to the sprawling deck that faces the ocean. It's there I escape, if only for a few moments. When I breathe in the salt-soaked air and scan the vastness of the sea, it's as if my soul hits a re-start button of sorts, setting the tone for my week.

Pausing a few minutes each day to worship God through the different senses adds a layer of depth to your beach experience, deepening your appreciation for God and His love for you. So when you arrive at your new surroundings today, take a moment to settle your soul in a holy hush, for nothing replenishes a parched soul like stillness.

BE STILL AND KNOW

"Be still and know that I am God." Psalm 46:10 NIV

Did you know that the term "be still" in Psalm 46:10 can also be translated "cease striving" or "let go, relax"? I don't know what stresses you left behind at home, but God does—and He's got it. Or does He?

Early on in my walk with Jesus, an older woman in my church shared how it's one thing to take my burdens to God, but it's another thing to leave them there. This is what God says to us every day: Cease striving. Let go—relax. Be still. Know—not just with your head but also with your heart, through experience—that I am God. I am for you, not against you. I'm here to give you hope in every circumstance. Leave your burdens here with Me.

Pause for a few moments before your vacation gets underway, and welcome the presence of the Lord. Open your hands; symbolically release whatever niggling circumstances you left behind at home. Be still and know.

Your heavenly Father longs to reveal Himself and His love for you. It's written across the sky. You hear it in music. You feel it when the wind sweeps across your face. You smell it in the scent of fresh rain and experience it when you come face-to-face with His goodness.

His love surrounds you.

PRAYER PAUSE

Heavenly Father,
Thank You for a safe arrival to this place You have provided for
my physical, emotional, and soul rest. You are a Father who wants
to be known by His children. You don't hide from me or play
games. You pursue me with an everlasting love. Thank You for the
variety of senses You created within me, enhancing my
appreciation of Your truths, Your character, and Your beauty.
Bring my soul to holy hushes this week as I stand in awe of You,
Father. Amen.

SUGGESTED GROCERY LIST

There are a couple of items that will enhance your sensory experiences later this week. If you're like me, you shop soon after arriving, so I want to share two things you may want to add to your grocery list:

- Snack-size resealable bags (I would suggest you

splurge for the name brand as they tend to have a stronger seal).

- A cluster of grapes (you'll enjoy these on Day 4).

~

To go out with the setting sun on an empty beach is to truly embrace your solitude.
— Jeanne Moreau

DAY ONE // PAUSE TO SEE

Heavenly Father,
Awaken my spiritual eyes to see You fully, in all Your glory.
Give me discernment to see beyond what my physical eyes
will allow.
Amen.

*B*efore daybreak, my dad and I slipped through the tightly sprung screened door without making a sound. With readied pockets and a flashlight, we made our way to the shore in search of sharks' teeth, one of the many things Dad once collected. A natural-born teacher, he enjoyed sharing his sage advice about ways to find one of the beach's most elusive treasures.

"To begin, look only for the shape of a shark's tooth," he said, bending down to lightly scratch through the myriad of shells deposited overnight by the ocean.

I mistook many shapes in the sand for sharks' teeth as a little girl. But like any good dad, he praised the many finds that at first glance appeared to be sharks' teeth but were instead imposters. Sensing my frustration, he didn't waste any time in sharing two more ways to tell the difference.

"Look closely at the top part. It should look different than the part with the point. Sharks have enamel on their teeth just like ours," he said, while gently prying my fingers open. Then he flipped my find over, revealing how the back part was hollow, rather than solid and flat like that of a shark's tooth.

Since then, I've honed my hunting skills to the point where I can now look past the mass of imposters staring back at me and see the treasures eagerly waiting to be placed in my pocket for safekeeping.

You and I *look* a lot—but do we really *see*?

BE STILL AND KNOW

"Lift up your eyes and look to the heavens: Who created all these? He who brings out the starry host one by one and calls forth each of them by name. Because of his great power and mighty strength, not one of them is missing." Isaiah 40:26 NIV

God says lift your eyes, look to the heavens. There you will see His love for you with your own eyes. Smatterings of stars dazzle the sky, displaying God's love for all to see.

Did you know that astronomers guesstimate there to be 100 billion stars in our galaxy alone? Our Creator not only spoke the stars into existence. He gave them a specific place in the galaxy to shine. And He named them. Not one star out of the 100 billion in existence is out of place. Not one has escaped its Maker's notice. *And neither have you.*

Take a few moments to move outside. Depending on the time you're reading this, choose one or both options:

Daytime: If possible, make your way to the beach. Or simply step outside and inhale the salty air. What do you see? Soak in the majesty of God's handiwork. Does something particular catch your eye? Is it the vastness of the sea? Seashells intricately designed by your Maker? Or maybe it's a sea gull swooping down to fetch its next meal?

Evening: Look up. What do you see written on the chalkboard sky above? Are the stars putting on a show, or did they take the night off? Is the moon visible, or is it disguised as a cloud?

God formed you but He didn't leave you there. He calls you by name. He knows you. He knows your strengths, your hardest struggles, and your purpose. So look up! There you will see an excerpt of God's love letter to you, with the full story spelled out in God's Word.

- How did you see God's love spelled out for you while outside?
- Has it been awhile since you've seen God's personal touch on your life? Sometimes we can be tempted to weigh that question based on what we physically see God doing in our lives. This can be deceptive, as God does not always choose to visibly display his work. It's during these times that you must engage your spiritual sight, trusting that you never escape your heavenly Father's sight. Pray for God to open both your physical and spiritual sight to see Him afresh this week.

Group Questions: Go to http://www.cathybaker.org/pauses-exclusive-content-beach (Password: pauses - beach)

PRAYER PAUSE

Heavenly Father, I praise You for the heavens that remind me every night of Your love. At times, I can't see the stars for the clouds, but they are there. When I can't see You at work in my life, help me to remember that You are near. Just as You are intimately acquainted with every star, so you are acquainted with me. You see me and love me. Amen.

≈

"ONE OF MY EARLIEST MEMORIES IS OF SEEING MY MOTHER IN HER BEACH CHAIR, READING A BOOK UNDER AN UMBRELLA BY THE WATER'S EDGE WHILE MY SISTERS AND I PLAYED BESIDE HER. OF ALL THE LIFE LESSONS SHE TAUGHT ME, THAT IS ONE OF MY FAVORITES: TO TAKE TIME AT THE PLACE I LOVE, RESTORE MY SPIRIT WITH BOOKS AND AND THE BEACH. "

-LUANNE RICE

DAY 2 // PAUSE TO INHALE

Heavenly Father,
Thank you for the ability to perceive my surroundings through the
sense of smell. It's a tremendous gift! One whiff can immediately
transport me back to a beautiful memory. Awaken my senses today
for Your glory.
Amen.

*B*eside the bed in the cottage where I stayed as a young girl stood a rickety bedside table. Over the table was a screened window. Before bedtime, my dad would crack it open several inches. The white, weathered paint that coated the windowsill protested every single time.

The warm earthy scent of damp sand meshed with salt-soaked breezes wafted through my window each night. It lulled me to sleep without fail.

BE STILL AND KNOW

Remember Mary, Lazarus' sister? She doused Jesus' feet with expensive perfume and wiped them with her hair. Only days earlier, Jesus had raised her brother Lazarus from the dead. Deep gratitude has a way of generating powerful worship.

As an only child it's hard to relate to the gratefulness Mary must have felt when Jesus raised her brother, but that doesn't mean I can't relate.

Years ago, I was a young single mom. The scent rising from my poor choices was anything but lovely. But all that changed one night in a tiny duplex, after I put my two little boys to bed. God's presence was palpable. He raised my sin-stained heart from the pit that night and gave me life. Gratitude spilled from my eyes in much the same way Mary's perfume must have spilled onto Jesus' feet.

"Then Mary took about a pint of pure nard, an expensive perfume; she poured it on Jesus' feet and wiped his feet with her hair. And the house was filled with the fragrance of the perfume." John 12:3 NIV

The perfume was a year's pay, but Mary's extravagant and daring display of love was impossible to measure by man's wages.

In those days, Jewish women rarely, if ever, let their hair down in public. It was downright scandalous. But Mary didn't allow man's rules or preconceived notions to limit the way she chose to express her love and gratitude for Jesus.

Take a few moments to step outside and close your eyes. Inhale deeply. Allow your surroundings to fully engage your senses.

What scents catch your attention?

- The whiff of salty breezes?
- Brine-laden winds blowing in from nearby marshlands?
- Tropical suntan lotion?

Are there any scents that carry you back to a specific place and time?

I can't help but wonder if this is what happened to Mary.

The same fragrance used to prepare her brother's body for burial only days earlier was now being used to show her devotion, love, and gratitude to the One who raised him from the dead. Her gratitude deepened, as did her faith, with each swipe of her hair, as she remembered Jesus' power and authority over the grave.

"Our lives are a Christ-like fragrance rising up to God." – 2 Corinthians 2:15 NLT

To some, this Christ-like fragrance we evoke is inviting. To others, it is repulsive. Either way, we worship at the feet of Jesus.

In the perfume industry the term "sillage" is used for the trail of scent a person leaves in her wake. When Mary left to go about life after wiping the perfume from Jesus' feet, the fragrance continued to linger in her long locks of hair. Her time with Jesus was evident to those around her.

Do others catch the scent of Christ after your time with Him?

Group Questions: Go to http://www.cathybak-er.org/pauses-exclusive-content-beach (Password: pauses - beach)

PRAYER PAUSE

Heavenly Father,
I desire to worship You in spirit and truth. May my actions mirror
my heart as I seek to live fully present in Your Spirit. Show me how
to be an extravagant worshipper! Infuse me with Your love, mercy,
and grace so that others may be drawn closer to You as a result.
Amen.

Extra: Consider buying a candle with a beach scent when you return home. During your holy hush time with God, light the candle as a simple reminder of His sweet presence.

～

"WHEN YOU GO THROUGH THE DEEP WATERS, I WILL BE
WITH YOU."
ISAIAH 43:2 NLT

DAY 3 // PAUSE TO LISTEN

Heavenly Father,
Thank you for this moment in time. With the clatter of a busy life
behind me, would you invade my heart and mind with the kind of
stillness that only Your Spirit can create? Today, as I focus my
attention on the gift of sound, fill my heart with gratitude for both
the Creator and his creation.
Amen.

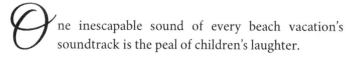ne inescapable sound of every beach vacation's soundtrack is the peal of children's laughter.

Amusement park rides, multiple scoops of Superman-flavored ice cream, family games of putt-putt, and riding waves to shore on Styrofoam surfboards all competed for our boys' attention during our beach vacations. But one destination stood out among the rest—the local arcade.

A cacophony of sounds assaulted the senses—chimes, beeps, bumper thumps, shrieks of laughter, and the racking of wooden skee-balls. But the boys' ultimate goal in playing was to have the games spit out enough tickets to redeem "parachute men"—small, green army men laced with string and tied to a plastic chute.

Along with their step-dad and grandfather, the boys, with hard-earned troops tightly clutched, would make their way to the top floor balcony of our condo. There, they would release them, one-by-one. The boys were thrilled to see where the wind would carry their brave little soldiers, as evidenced by the laughter heard long after the parachute men took flight.

Our now-adult sons delight in the giddy sounds their own children make when they jump waves, scoop wet sand into buckets for sandcastles, and run carefree into the wind.

Few things rival the sound of a child immersed in joy—except, perhaps the sound of your name when spoken by someone you love.

BE STILL AND KNOW

"Then the disciples went back to their homes, but Mary [Magdeline] stood outside the tomb crying. As she wept, she bent over to look into the tomb and saw two angels in white, seated where Jesus' body had been, one at the head and the other at the foot.

They asked her, "Woman, why are you crying?"

"They have taken my Lord away," she said, "and I don't know where they have put him." At this, she turned around and saw Jesus standing there but she did not realize that it was Jesus.

"Woman," he said, "why are you crying? Who is it you are looking for?"

Thinking he was the gardener, she said, "Sir if you have carried him away, tell me where you have put him, and I will get him."

Jesus said to her, "Mary."

She turned toward him and cried out in Aramaic, "Rabboni!" (which means Teacher)."
John 20:10-16 NIV

Mary Magdalene, the woman from whom Jesus had once cast out seven demons, was the first person to the tomb on that glorious morning we celebrate as Easter. As soon as she saw the stone removed, she ran to Simon Peter and John. After they witnessed the empty tomb, they returned to their homes—but Mary stayed. She stood outside the tomb in tears. There, she would come face to face with her Lord, but it wasn't His face she recognized. It was His voice.

Can you hear the tenderness as He speaks her name? We see no doubt or hesitation on her part as she responded to Him. She knew the timbre of her Savior's voice because she had spent time with Him.

Allow this truth to linger while you step outside. If possible, take a stroll on the beach. Absorb all the sounds in your particular surroundings. What do you hear?

- The heavy thump of a runner as her heels hit the wet sand?
- The clinking of seashells in pockets?
- Small planes with ad banners buzzing across the sky?

- Fishermen boasting over the size of their catch that day?

Some things are easy to hear—others, not so much.

Sometimes God's voice is as clear as letters written in wet sand. And then there are times His voice seems distant.

Mary Magdalene heard Jesus speak when she traveled with Him and the disciples. But she didn't simply hear. She listened.

Put yourself in Mary's place that day outside the empty tomb. As you bend over to look in the tomb you see two angels in white, seated where Jesus' body once laid. You turn around and there stands Jesus. You don't recognize Him. But then He calls out *your* name. Do you recognize His voice?

God still speaks today. He speaks through His Word. But, while never contradicting scripture, He also speaks in additional ways such as prayer, other Christ-followers, nature, and music. Do you hear Him? Or do other things drown out His voice?

We may not hear an audible voice until we reach heaven, but His desire to speak to us—to speak our name—has not lessened. The next time you read scripture and the Spirit quickens within you, there's your "name". Like Mary, it requires not only hearing the Word but also listening to what it says.

Group Questions: Go to http://www.cathybaker.org/pauses-exclusive-content-beach (Password: pauses - beach)

PRAYER PAUSE

Heavenly Father,
No sound on earth rivals that of your voice. Even when your words
are difficult to hear, I am assured through your promises that they
are grounded in love, mercy, and forgiveness. I know based on your
Word that you will never speak words of condemnation to me.
Thank you for your Spirit who helps me to discern what I hear and
receive. Forgive me when I allow anything to compete with your
voice. Speak, Lord. I am listening. Amen.

~

"THE SEA IS HIS, FOR IT WAS HE WHO MADE IT, AND HIS HANDS FORMED THE DRY LAND." PSALM 95:5 NIV

DAY 4 // PAUSE TO TASTE

Heavenly Father,
Your goodness surrounds me at every turn.
Even on days when clouds are as heavy as my heart
I trust your loving kindness toward me. Not one inkling of pain –
physically, emotionally, or spiritually – escapes Your attention.
Every moment of my life is filtered through your hands of love,
mercy, and grace.
May I taste and see You afresh today.
Amen.

Some of my best childhood memories trace back to a pink beach house trimmed in white, propped as pretty as you please on the Myrtle Beach seaside. Dark pine-paneled walls, faux leather furniture with beefy arm rests, an outdoor shower in addition to the interior one, and oh, those linoleum floors! But the best part of my summer family beach trips was my grandmother's cooking. While everyone else in the family packed bathing suits and sandals, Ma-Ma was busy packing cooking utensils and fresh corn from the Upstate.

The aromas that wafted through that pink summerhouse mingled perfectly with the sea salt breezes, to create unforgettable memories.

Is there a particular food you associate with your vacation trips to the beach?

BE STILL AND KNOW

Psalm 34:8 says, "Taste and see that the Lord is good." To taste something implies eating. When food is eaten, it's digested, and in a very real sense it becomes a part of your body. To taste of the Lord is to experience Him in every facet of life by faith. No one else can digest your food for you; in the same way, no one else can experience the Lord for you. Only you can taste the sweetness of God's goodness for yourself. It's no secret, however, that not all of your days will be sweet. In fact, some will be downright bitter. Jesus knows something about a bitter tasting cup.

"Then the mother of James and John, the sons of Zebedee, came to Jesus with her sons. She knelt respectfully to ask a favor. "What is your request?" he asked.
She replied, "In your Kingdom, please let my two sons sit in places of honor next to you, one on your right and the other on your left."
But Jesus answered by saying to them, "You don't know what you are asking! Are you able to drink from the bitter cup of suffering I am about to drink?" Matthew 20:22 NLT

Jesus knew what lay ahead and yet it says in Hebrews 12:2, *"For the joy set before him he endured the cross, scorning its shame, and sat down at the right hand of the throne of God."*

When you look back on past "bitter-cup" days, can you taste the remnants of God's love, mercy, and goodness in that situation? Pause for a moment and thank God for never leaving or forsaking you. (Hebrews 13:5 NIV)

Hold a cluster of grapes (or imagine them if you don't have them on hand). Can you tell if the grapes are sweet or sour from simply looking at them? You can guess as to their sweetness, but it's not until you taste them for yourself that you know for certain.

Note that David doesn't say, "Taste and see *if* the Lord is good." David knows by experience, both sweet and bitter, that God is good because he has personally relied on him, witnessing first-hand his protection and faithfulness. Even in those times when God disciplined David, ultimately he saw the goodness of the Lord.

Spend a few moments listing in a journal (or on a paper napkin!) the specific ways you have personally tasted and seen God's goodness in both pleasant and difficult ways. Then consider how you can savor His goodness, and fully appreciate His ways—whether you see them or not.

You can taste God's goodness in your life as much as you can taste your favorite food at the beach. It's that real, that good.

Group Questions: Go to http://www.cathybaker.org/pauses-exclusive-content-beach (Password: pauses - beach)

PRAYER PAUSE

Heavenly Father,
Oh, how sweet are Your words and ways toward me. They taste

sweeter than honey. Your goodness is evident throughout the generations. I'm grateful I can experience You for myself. I don't have to rely on anyone else to be a taste-tester. Even on days that are bitter to the tongue, Your goodness reigns. Thank You for taking my bitter cup and joyfully enduring the cross on my behalf. I have tasted of your goodness and I am changed forever as a result.

Amen.

~

"Then God said, "Let the waters below the heavens be gathered into one place, and let the dry land appear"; and it was so. God called the dry land earth, and the gathering of the waters He called seas; and God saw that it was good." Genesis 1:9-10 NASB

DAY 5 // PAUSE TO TOUCH

Heavenly Father,
I praise You today for being the Creator of all things sensory.
Through Jesus, the loneliest, most ostracized people on earth were
touched—physically and spiritually. Even your Word was breathed
into being, touched by your holy exhaling power. May I never
underestimate the power of this gift, the touch.
Amen.

*W*aves scared me as a young girl. I tended to stick close to shore with the shells, sand, and the occasional shark's tooth. The only time I ventured out to sea (all 20 feet of it) was when my dad took me by the hand and led me out beyond the first crest to jump waves. When a larger one began building, he lifted me up over his head, singlehandedly taking on the wave. His tight but loving grip put my fears on notice that I was safe now and they could go away. And they did.

Today will include a walk to the sandy shore—so tuck a

CATHY BAKER

beach blanket under your arm, along with 2 small re-sealable bags, and head outside. I'll meet you there.

BE STILL AND KNOW

As you sit on the beach, fling off those flip-flops. Allow your toes to tickle the soft sand surrounding your towel. As you settle in, scoop up a handful of sand and study it for a few moments. Can you imagine trying to count the vast number of sand particles in your palm, much less over all the earth? And yet, God tells you in Psalm 139:17-18 that his thoughts concerning you (yes, you!) outnumber them.

> *"How difficult it is for me to fathom your thoughts about me,*
> *O God!*
> *How vast is their sum total! If I tried to count them,*
> *they would outnumber the grains of sand." Psalm 139:17-18 NET*

Have you ever considered what those thoughts might be? Here are two to consider:

"For I know the plans I have for you," declares the LORD, "plans to prosper you and not to harm you, plans to give you hope and a future." Jeremiah 29:11 NIV

"Therefore, there is now no condemnation for those who are in Christ Jesus..." Romans 8:1 NIV

Try to grasp the reality that the one true living God has you on His mind at all times. You are never out of His sight or His care.

What does it mean to you that your heavenly Father has you on His mind every nanosecond of the day? On the days when you feel lonely, abandoned, or depressed, how can claiming this truth for yourself encourage your soul?

As your toes continue to sink into the sand, allow the truth of God's Word to penetrate your heart and mind. At times you may feel forgotten by God, but He doesn't forget you for one granular moment.

Scoop up a handful of dry sand and place it in the small resealable bag. This bag is yours. If you know someone who may need a reminder of God's love back home, fill up another one. (If you don't have bags, take a close-up picture of the sand to serve as a reminder.)

Look closely at the sand in your bag as you read today's verse once more:

"How difficult it is for me to fathom your thoughts about me,
O God!
How vast is their sum total! If I tried to count them,
they would outnumber the grains of sand." Psalm 139:17-18 NET

I ended a Bible study many years ago by handing out snack bags full of dry sand with this verse written on it. Just recently, a woman who attended that study mentioned how her bag of sand stays in her bedside table to serve as a daily reminder of God's personal care for her. You may want to consider the same when you return home. Keep it nearby or perhaps place your sand in a glass container for all to see. It could be a life-altering conversation starter!

Allow the simple grains of sand to serve as your own personal reminder of God's unceasing, loving thoughts toward *you*. Because, let's face it, we all have those days when we're tempted to believe otherwise.

Group Questions: Go to http://www.cathybaker.org/pauses-exclusive-content-beach (Password: pauses - beach)

PRAYER PAUSE

Heavenly Father,
I can't begin to comprehend the vastness of Your love—and Your thoughts—toward me. Who am I? Because of Jesus, I can answer in full confidence that I am Yours and You are Mine. When circumstances threaten to kidnap this confidence, remind me of the countless grains of sand that ran through my fingers and toes today. Thank You for this tangible reminder of Your love for me. Amen.

~

"I AM VERY FOND OF THE OYSTER SHELL. IT IS HUMBLE AND
AWKWARD AND UGLY. IT IS SLATE-COLORED AND
UNSYMMETRICAL. ITS FORM IS NOT PRIMARILY BEAUTIFUL BUT
FUNCTIONAL. I MAKE FUN OF ITS KNOBBINESS. SOMETIMES I
RESENT ITS BURDENS AND EXCRESCENCES. BUT ITS TIRELESS
ADAPTABILITY AND TENACITY DRAW MY ASTONISHED
ADMIRATION AND SOMETIMES EVEN MY TEARS. AND IT IS
COMFORTABLE IN ITS FAMILIARITY, ITS HOMELINESS, LIKE OLD
GARDEN GLOVES WHEN HAVE MOLDED THEMSELVES PERFECTLY
TO THE SHAPE OF THE HAND. I DO NOT LIKE TO PUT IT DOWN. I
WILL NOT WANT TO LEAVE IT."
— ANNE MORROW LINDBERGH, *GIFT FROM THE SEA*

DEPARTURE DAY // PAUSE FOR A FRESH START

Heavenly Father,
Thank you for revealing Yourself to me in precious and unique
ways this week. As I prepare to head home today, I pray not only
for the protection for a safe trip but also for protection of the
knowledge revealed to me this week through your Word and the
wonder discovered through my five senses.
Amen.

Some of my earliest memories of family beach trips involved packing the car the night before our departure. Daybreak had nothing on us! We headed out early for our four-hour trip home. I suppose the desire to beat daybreak is genetically inclined. Both of our boys, now adults with families of their own, pack up their vehicles at night, and load up drowsy little ones in pitch darkness the following morning.

BE STILL AND KNOW

It's never easy to say goodbyes to family or friends we may not see for a while, or pull away from a rental where life-long memories were created, but a fresh start awaits you at home.

"It's not what you look at that matters, it's what you see." Henry David Thoreau

This is true for all of life, right? When you embrace and engage your God-given senses, you are able to tune into the nuances of life you may have missed before.

You may not see a vast ocean at home
but
only look up at the sky ablaze with stars to be reminded of the personal God you love and serve. He gave each star a name and a place. He does the same for you. You are where you are for a purpose. Shine, sister, shine!

You may not catch the scent of salt-laden breezes at home
but
you are reminded that the fragrance you carry from your time with Christ is heavier and sweeter than anything the wind carries across the sea.

You may not hear the cry of a seagull when you return home
but
you know there is no sound like that of your Savior's voice. Especially when He tenderly whispers your name.

You may not taste fresh seafood at home
but
you can taste God's goodness toward you and those you love —even on the toughest days.

You may not be able to touch fine white grains of sand
at home
but
you are confident that you are always on your Maker's mind.
And on those days when doubt tries to creep in, you can pull
out your bag of sand and start counting.

Was there a particular day or sensory experience that resonated with you this week? Why do you think this particular day resonated more than the others? Is there a deeper truth that God wants to reveal to you?

What one attribute of God can you praise Him for right now, despite the busyness of departure day?

PRAYER PAUSE

Oh, Father!
Thank You for this week of respite and refreshment. I leave today longing to know You more, longing to spend time with You when I return home. I praise You for revealing Yourself to me through the different senses You created within me.
Continue to awaken me to You, Your ways, Your love, and Your Word.
Amen.

KEEPERS

[AWARD WINNING POEM BY CATHY BAKER]

Sometimes in July

I rise early,

Eager to collect

Worthy tokens

From the sea—

Whole, lovely,

Unblemished ones—

Keepers,

If you will.

Keepers ride

Wave trains,

Traveling past broken,

Marred, faded shells.

How to choose?

Sculpted skeletons

With pristine

Custom-fit walls

Pirouette like ballerinas

On display.

A tender undertow

Emerges as

Scarred, fragmented,

Slighted tokens

Hold my glance.

Flaws reveal

Tumbling ways,

Vulnerabilities

Displayed for

The choosing.

Jagged edges

Press into tender places,

Releasing the reality

Of my own

Tumbling ways.

Brokenness

Emerges as wholeness

Ushering in

Unexpected grace.

Sometimes in July

I rise early,

Eager to collect

Worthy tokens

From the sea

Scarred, fragmented,

Slighted ones—

Keepers,

If you will.

THANK YOU

Dear Reader,

Before you go, I'd like to say thank you for purchasing *Pauses for the Vacationing Soul: A Sensory-Based Devotional Guide for the Beach*.

I pray the Lord used this guide to enhanced your vacation for His ultimate glory.

If you were blessed by what you read, would you consider taking a moment to leave a review for this book on Amazon? Thank you!

A GIFT FOR YOU

Email Cathy at tea4thee@charter.net to receive a download-able beach-inspired coloring page designed specifically for this book as my way of saying thank-you for your purchase.

By: Britt Leigh // Design & Marketing Studio

ACKNOWLEDGMENTS

~

Because even the tiniest of books requires the help of those with the largest of hearts. Thank you:

Brian, for your unceasing encouragement, support, and love.

Dee Dee Parker, my fellow sweet pea in the strange little pod.

Edie, my mentor, prayer partner, and faithful friend.

Lori Roeleveld, the greatest giant-slayer this side of heaven.

Susan Stilwell (Fistbump Media), who goes the extra mile to make my website dreams come true.

My critique group--Marcia, Beth, and Carol--who I'm honored to call friends above all else.

The God-loving, beach-going, book launch team that rocks!

And to my dad—thank you for providing a lifetime of beautiful beach memories for our family.

ABOUT THE AUTHOR

Cathy Baker is an award-winning writer and author of **Pauses for the Vacationing Soul: A Sensory-Based Devotional Guide for the Beach** as well as **Pauses for the Vacationing Soul: A Sensory-Based Devotional Guide for the Mountains.** As a twenty-five year veteran Bible instructor, she's led hundreds of studies and workshops. She's also contributed to numerous anthologies and publications, including *Chicken Soup for the Soul, The Upper Room,* and Focus on the Family's *Thriving Family.* In addition, her poetry can be found in several popular anthologies. She and her husband, Brian, live in the foothills of the Carolinas where she one day hopes to raise Pygmy goats.

Connect with Cathy online at www.cathybaker.org where you'll find her blog Cultivating Creativity.

For more information:
tea4thee@charter.net

ALSO BY CATHY BAKER

Pauses for the Vacationing Soul: A Sensory-Based Devotional Guide for the Mountains

Coming Soon:

- Pauses for the Vacationing Soul: A Sensory-Based Devotional Guide for the Lake

- Pauses for the Vacationing Soul: A Sensory-Based Devotional Guide for Camping

- Holiday Sensory-Based Devotional Guides

Made in the USA
Coppell, TX
26 August 2022